xBiog Linco.A Linco.A

Lincoln, Abraham,
 1809-1865.
The first book edition
 of The Gettysburg
 [1963]

The
GETTYSBURG ADDRESS
The
SECOND INAUGURAL

The First Book Edition of

The
GETTYSBURG ADDRESS
The
SECOND INAUGURAL

Abraham Lincoln

ILLUSTRATED BY LEONARD EVERETT FISHER

INTRODUCED BY CARL SANDBURG

FRANKLIN WATTS, INC.
575 Lexington Avenue, New York 22

Library of Congress Catalog Card Number 63-7152
Illustrations © 1963 by Franklin Watts, Inc.

PRINTED IN THE UNITED STATES OF AMERICA

2 3 4 5

The Gettysburg Address

Introduction

A PRINTED INVITATION NOTIFIED Lincoln that on Thursday, November 19, 1863, exercises would be held for the dedication of a National Soldiers' Cemetery at Gettysburg. . . .

Lincoln, in reply to the printed invitation, sent word to the commissioners that he would be present at the ceremonies. The commissioners then considered whether the President should be asked to deliver an address. Clark E. Carr of Galesburg, Illinois, representing his state on the Board of Commissioners, noted that the decision of the board to invite Lincoln to speak was "an afterthought." . . .

When Lincoln boarded the train for Gettysburg November 18, his best chum in the world, Tad, lay sick abed and the doctors not sure what ailed him. The mother still mourned for Willie and was hysterical about Tad. But the President felt imperative duty called him to Gettysburg. . . .

At dinner in the Wills home that evening Lincoln met Edward Everett, Governor Curtin and others. About 11 o'clock, he gathered his sheets of paper and went next door for a half-hour with his Secretary of State. Whether Seward made slight or material alterations in the text was known only to Lincoln and Seward. It was midnight or later that Lincoln went to sleep. He slept better for having a telegram from Stanton reporting there was no real war news and "On inquiry Mrs. Lincoln informs me that your son is better this evening."

Fifteen thousand, some said 30,000 or 50,000, people

[2]

were on Cemetery Hill for the exercises next day when the procession from Gettysburg arrived afoot and horseback—members of the U.S. Government, the Army and Navy, governors of states, mayors of cities, a regiment of troops, hospital corps, telegraph company representatives, Knights Templar, Masonic Fraternity, Odd Fellows and other benevolent associations, the press, fire departments, citizens of Pennsylvania and other states. At ten o'clock Lincoln in a black suit, high silk hat and white gloves came out of the Wills residence, mounted a horse, and held a reception on horseback. At 11 the parade began to move. Clark E. Carr, just behind the President, believed he noticed that the President sat erect and looked majestic to begin with and then got to thinking so that his body leaned forward, his arms hung limp, his head bent far down....

He took out his own manuscript from a coat pocket, put on his steel-bowed glasses, stirred in his chair, looked over the manuscript, and put it back in his pocket. The Baltimore Glee Club finished. Ward Hill Lamon rose and spoke the words, "The President of the United States," who rose, and holding in one hand the two sheets of paper at which he occasionally glanced, delivered the address in his high-pitched and clear-carrying voice. The Cincinnati Commercial reporter wrote, "The President rises slowly, draws from his pocket a paper, and, when commotion subsides, in a sharp, unmusical treble voice, reads the brief and pithy remarks." Hay wrote in his diary, "The President, in

Introduction

a firm, free way, with more grace than is his wont, said his half dozen words of consecration." Charles Hale of the Boston Advertiser, *also officially representing Governor Andrew of Massachusetts, had notebook and pencil in hand, took down the slow-spoken words of the President:*

Introduction

From ABRAHAM LINCOLN: THE PRAIRIE YEARS AND THE WAR YEARS, One-Volume Edition, by Carl Sandburg, copyright, 1926, by Harcourt, Brace & World, Inc., copyright, 1954, by Carl Sandburg. Reprinted by permission of the publishers.

The Gettysburg Address

FOURSCORE AND SEVEN years ago our fathers brought forth on this continent a new nation, conceived in liberty, and dedicated to the proposition that all men are created equal. Now we are engaged in a great civil war, testing whether that nation, or any nation so conceived and so dedicated, can long endure. We are met on a great battlefield of that war. We have come to dedicate a portion of that field as a final resting place for those who here gave their lives that that nation might live. It is altogether fitting and proper that we should do this. But in a larger sense we cannot dedicate, we cannot consecrate, we cannot hallow this ground. The brave men, living and dead, who struggled here, have consecrated it far above our poor power to add or detract. The world will little note, nor long remember, what we say here; but it can never forget

The Gettysburg Address

"*Now we are engaged in a great civil war . . .*"

The Gettysburg Address

what they did here. It is for us, the living, rather to be dedicated here to the unfinished work which they who fought here have thus far so nobly advanced. It is rather for us to be here dedicated to the great task remaining before us, that from these honored dead we take increased devotion to that cause for which they gave the last full measure of devotion; that we here highly resolve that these dead shall not have died in vain; that this nation, under God, shall have a new birth of freedom, and that government of the people, by the people, and for the people, shall not perish from the earth.

The Gettysburg Address

"... that from these honored dead we take increased devotion to that cause..."

"*At this second appearing to take the oath of the Presidential office . . .*"

The Second Inaugural

Introduction

On March 4, 1865, hours before noon, Lincoln in a Senate wing room considered and signed bills. A parade on Pennsylvania Avenue from the White House to the Capitol moved in a light drizzle of rain and cold, gusty winds. A muddy paste coated the sidewalks lined with spectators. On one wagon platform printers from the Typographical Society, a labor union, ran a hand press and scattered programs of the day's events. A battalion of Negro troops in Union Army blue marched, and the Negro Grand Lodge of Odd Fellows.

Toward noon flocks of women streamed around the Capitol, "crinoline smashed, skirts bedaubed, velvet and laces streaked with mud." And the women, noted Brooks, kept unfailing good nature though "such another dirty crowd probably never was seen." In the galleries women in wide crinoline "filled the seats like a cloud," not a man finding a seat. "Diamonds flashed, feathers nodded (damply), bright faces gleamed, and the noise of feminine tongues was like a swarm of bees." Senator Foot of Vermont rapped his gavel for order but "a rippling storm of small talk in the galleries went on."

Invited notables trod to their reserved seats. Noah Brooks wrote of Mrs. Lincoln, attended by Senator Anthony, seated in the Diplomatic Gallery, and a buzz when the Justices of the Supreme Court entered in their black robes. A few stray governors came in, then the Diplomatic Corps, in gold lace, feathers and white pantaloons. One ambassador

[16]

had to unbutton himself to get his feet on the floor. Members of the House moved in at noon, then the Cabinet. . . .

The procession to the Capitol portico formed and moved. The drizzle of rain had stopped. "A tremendous shout, prolonged and loud, arose from the surging ocean of humanity," wrote Noah Brooks. The President with invited notables took the platform. Then the sergeant at arms of the Senate arose and with raised hands got the crowd still. And Abraham Lincoln, rising tall, gaunt and outstanding, stepped forward to read his inaugural address. Applause roared, again and again was repeated, and finally died far away on the outer fringe of the throng.

In the silence almost profound the audience now listened. Seldom had a President been so short-spoken about the issues of so grave an hour. He read his carefully and deliberately prepared address:

Introduction

From ABRAHAM LINCOLN: THE PRAIRIE YEARS AND THE WAR YEARS, One-Volume Edition, by Carl Sandburg, copyright, 1926, by Harcourt, Brace & World, Inc., copyright, 1954, by Carl Sandburg. Reprinted by permission of the publishers.

[17]

Fellow-Countrymen:

The Second Inaugural

AT THIS SECOND APPEARING to take the oath of the Presidential office there is less occasion for an extended address than there was at the first. Then a statement somewhat in detail of a course to be pursued seemed fitting and proper. Now, at the expiration of four years, during which public declarations have been constantly called forth on every point and phase of the great contest which still absorbs the attention and engrosses the energies of the nation, little that is new could be presented. The progress of our arms, upon which all else chiefly depends, is as well known to the public as to myself, and it is, I trust, reasonably satisfactory and encouraging to all. With high hope for the future, no prediction in regard to it is ventured.

On the occasion corresponding to this four years ago all thoughts were anxiously directed to an impending

The Second Inaugural

[19]

"*The progress of our arms . . . is as well known to the public as to myself . . .*"

The Second Inaugural

civil war. All dreaded it, all sought to avert it. While the inaugural address was being delivered from this place, devoted altogether to *saving* the Union without war, insurgent agents were in the city seeking to *destroy* it without war — seeking to dissolve the Union and divide effects by negotiation. Both parties deprecated war, but one of them would *make* war rather than let the nation survive, and the other would *accept*

" . . . and the war came."

The Second Inaugural

war rather than let it perish, and the war came.

One-eighth of the whole population were colored slaves, not distributed generally over the Union, but localized in the southern part of it. These slaves constituted a peculiar and powerful interest. All knew that this interest was somehow the cause of the war. To strengthen, perpetuate and extend this interest was the object for which the insurgents would

[24]

rend the Union even by war, while the Government claimed no right to do more than to restrict the territorial enlargement of it. Neither party expected for the war the magnitude or the duration which it has already attained. Neither anticipated that the *cause* of the conflict might cease with or even before the conflict itself should cease. Each looked for an easier triumph, and a result less fundamental and astounding. Both read

The Second Inaugural

"One-eighth of the whole population were colored slaves . . ."

The Second Inaugural

the same Bible and pray to the same God, and each invokes His aid against the other. It may seem strange that any men should dare to ask a just God's assistance in wringing their bread from the sweat of other men's faces, but let us judge not, that we be not judged. The prayers of both could not be answered. That of neither has been answered fully. The Almighty has His own purposes. "Woe unto the world because of

"... the woe due to those by whom the offense came ..."

The Second Inaugural

offenses; for it must needs be that offenses come, but woe to that man by whom the offense cometh." If we shall suppose that American slavery is one of those offenses which, in the providence of God, must needs come, but which, having continued through His appointed time, He now wills to remove, and that He gives to both North and South this terrible war as the woe due to those by whom the offense came, shall we discern therein any departure from those divine attributes which the believers in a living God always ascribe to Him? Fondly do we hope, fervently do we pray, that this mighty scourge of war may speedily pass away. Yet, if God wills that it continue until all the wealth piled by the bondsman's two hundred and fifty years of unrequited toil shall be sunk, and until every drop of blood drawn with the lash shall be paid by another drawn with

The Second Inaugural

" . . . *this mighty scourge of war* . . . "

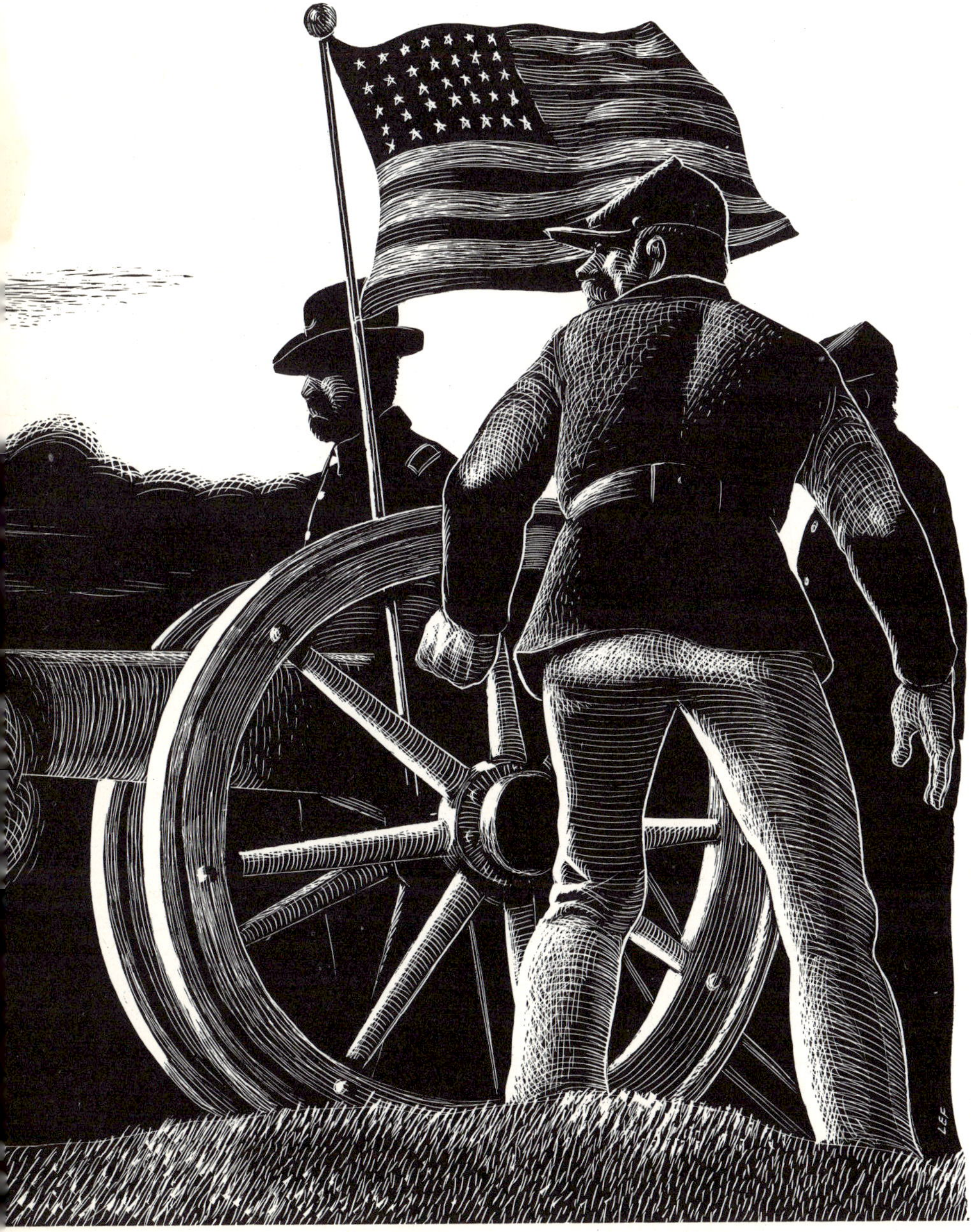
LEF

The Second Inaugural

the sword, as was said three thousand years ago, so still it must be said "the judgments of the Lord are true and righteous altogether."

With malice toward none, with charity for all, with firmness in the right as God gives us to see the right, let us strive on to finish the work we are in, to bind up the nation's wounds, to care for him who shall have borne the battle and for his widow and his orphan, to do all which may achieve and cherish a just and lasting peace among ourselves and with all nations.

The Second Inaugural

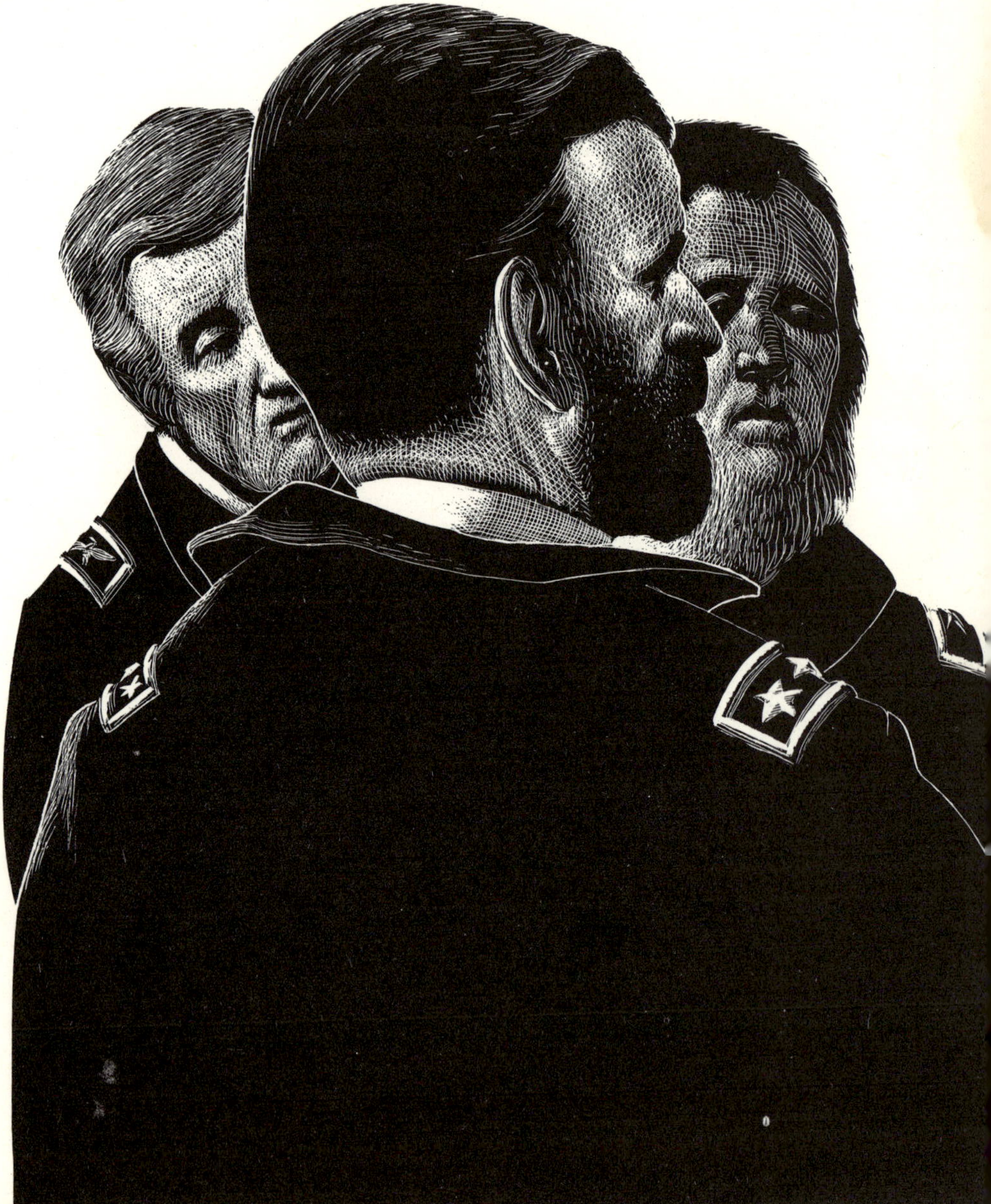

"With malice toward none, with charity for all . . ."

EVANSTON PUBLIC LIBRARY
1703 ORRINGTON AVENUE
EVANSTON, ILLINOIS 60201

LEONARD EVERETT FISHER was born in New York City and received his Bachelor and Master of Fine Arts degrees at the Yale Art School. He has been awarded the Weir Prize, the Winchester Fellowship, and the Pulitzer Art Prize. In recent years he has become an extremely successful and sought-after illustrator of children's books. Among the books he has illustrated are *The First Book of the American Revolution*, *The First Book of New England*, *The First Book of the Constitution*, *The First Book Edition of The Man Without a Country*, *America, America, America*, *The First Book Edition of The Declaration of Independence*, *The First Book Edition of A Message to Garcia* and *Patriotism, Patriotism, Patriotism*.

The text of this edition of The Gettysburg Address and the Second Inaugural has been composed on the Monotype in Bembo.

Composed by Philmac Typographers, Inc., New York

Printed by Polygraphic Company of America, Inc., New York

Bound by H. Wolff Book Manufacturing Company, Inc., New York

DESIGNED BY BERNARD KLEIN

FIRST BOOKS
Complete Check List

Series No.	Quantity	TITLE	Author	Listings	Grade Reading Level
68		Atlas	C S Hammond & Co	A sl L	3-4
22		Africa	Hughes	A sl L CS	4-7
140		Air	Knight	A sl L	4 up
1		Airplanes	Bendick	A sl L C CS	3-6
76		American History	Commager	A sl L C CS	4 up
11		The American Revolution	Morris	A sl L C CS	5 up
158		Ancient Bible Lands	Robinson	New Publication	
134		Ancient Egypt	Robinson	A L	4 up
110		Ancient Greece	Robinson	A L	4 up
150		Ancient Mesopotamia and Persia Robinson		A L	4 up
99		Ancient Rome	Robinson	A L	4 up
73		The Antarctic	Icenhower	A L C	4-7
77		Archaeology	Kubie	A sl L C CS	4 up
135		Architecture	Moore	A sl L	4 up
104		Astronomy	Grey	A L	4 up
107		Australia	Kaula	L	4-7
5		Automobiles	Bendick	A sl L C CS	3-5
44		The Ballet	Streatfeild	A sl CS	4-7
148		Barbarian Invaders	Sobol	A	5 up
14		Baseball	Brewster	A sl L C CS	3-5
94		Basketball	Schiffer	A sl L C	4-8
4		Bees	Tibbets	A L C CS	3-6
98		Bells	Fletcher	L CS	2-4
18		Birds	Williamson	A sl L C CS	3-6
2		Boats	Gossett	A L CS	2-4
101		Boys' Cooking	Beim	A sl L C CS	4 up
149		Brazil	Sheppard	A	4 up
43		Bridges	Peet	A L C CS	3-7
6		Bugs	Williamson	A sl L C CS H	3-5
153		California Gold Rush	Havighurst	A L	4-7
65		Canada	C & M Lineaweaver	A L C	4-6
139		Cartoons for Kids	Fenner		2-5
111		Cats	Taber	A sl L C	3-6
54		Caves	E Hamilton	A sl L C	4-6
45		Chess	Leeming	A sl L C CS H	5 up
173		The China Clippers	Rich	New Publication	
146		Christmas Joy	Wilson	A L	1-3
105		Civil War Land Battles	Dupuy	A sl L C	5 up
137		Civil War Naval Actions	Dupuy	A sl L	5 up
29		Codes and Ciphers	S & B Epstein	A sl L C CS H	3-5
95		Color	Paschel	A L C CS	5 up
157		Comunist China	Kinmond	New Publication	
108		The Congo	McDonnell	L	3-6
9		Congress	Coy	A sl L C H	5 up
47		Conservation	F C Smith	A sl L C CS	4-7
85		The Constitution	Morris	A sl L C CS	5 up
40		Cotton	Rogers	A L C CS	4-6
13		Cowboys	Brewster	A sl L C	4 up
10		Dogs	Taber	A L C CS	3-5
39		Dolls	H Hoke	A sl L C	1-3
88		Drawing	Slobodkin	A sl L C	6 up
96		The Early Settlers	Rich	A sl L C	4-6
81		The Earth	Sevrey	A L C	5 up
42		Electricity	S & B Epstein	A sl L C CS	4-8
83		England	Streatfeild	A L C CS	4-7
26		Eskimos	Brewster	A sl L C CS	3-5
79		Fairy Tales	Abell		3 up
25		Festivals	Reck	A L C	3-6
21		Firemen	Brewster	A L	3-5
69		Food	Scheib	A L C CS	3-5
87		Football	Schiffer	A sl L C	3 up
92		France	Gottlieb	A sl L C	4-7
61		Gardening	Kirkus	A sl L C	4-6
122		Ghana	Lobsenz	A sl L	4-7
155		Glaciers	Marcus	A L	4 up
60		Glass	S & B Epstein	A L C CS	3-5
48		Hawaii	S & B Epstein	A L C CS	4-6
62		Holidays	Burnett	A L C	3-5
8		Horses	McMeekin	A sl L C CS	5 up
129		How to Fix It	Bendick-Berk	A sl L	3 up
143		Human Senses	Liberty	A sl L	4 up
66		India	Hahn	L C CS	4-7
103		The Indian Wars	Morris	A	4 up
15		Indians (American)	Brewster	A L C CS	2-6
41		Israel	Kubie	A sl L C CS	4-7
89		Italy	S & B Epstein	A sl L C CS	4-7
30		Japan	Mears	A L C CS	4-7
58		Jazz	Hughes	A L C CS H	7 up
19		Jokes	Chrystie	A L C CS	3-6
130		Kings	Newton	L	3-6
172		Language & How To Use It	Applegate	New Publication	
159		Legendary Beings	Jacobson	New Publication	
74		Letter Writing	Jacobson	A L C CS	4-6
160		Light	Harrison	New Publication	
152		Machines	Buehr	A	3-6
46		Magic	Stoddard	A sl L C CS	3-5
75		Mammals	Williamson	A sl L C CS H	4 up
90		Maps and Globes	S & B Epstein	A sl L C CS	4-6
125		Measurement	S & B Epstein	L	4-6
102		Medieval Man	Sobol	A sl	4 up
123		The Mediterranean	Gottlieb	A L	4-7
63		Mexico	S & B Epstein	A L C H	4-7
35		Microbes	Lewis	A sl L C CS H	4 up
116		Mining	Markun	A L	3-6
51		Music	Norman	A sl L C CS	3-6
128		Mythical Beasts	Jacobson	A L	3-5
67		Mythology	Elgin	A sl L CS	4 up
113		National Monuments	Lobsenz	A L	3 up
115		National Parks	Lobsenz	A L	3 up
27		Negroes	Hughes	A sl L C CS	4 up
154		Netherlands	Cohn	A	4 up
12		New England	Rich	A L CS H	4-6
119		New World Explorers	Rich	A L	4-6
131		New Zealand	Kaula	A	4 up
72		Norse Legends	Elgin	L	4-6
16		Nurses	Elting	A sl L C CS	3-5
133		Ocean	Epstein	A L	4 up
109		The Oregon Trail	Havighurst	A L C	3-7
118		Paintings	Moore	A sl L C	4 up
151		Pakistan	Bothwell	A L	4 up
84		The Panama Canal	Markun	A sl L C CS	4 up
50		Photography	J Hoke	A sl L C CS H	5 up
142		Physical Fitness	Walsh	A L	4 up
97		Pioneers	Havighurst		4-8
38		Plants	Dickinson	A C CS	4 up
37		Poetry	Peterson	A sl L C CS	3-6
53		Prehistoric Animals	Dickinson	A sl L C CS	4-7
28		Presidents	Coy	A L CS	4-6
64		Printing	S & B Epstein	A sl L C CS H	5 up
114		Public Libraries	Graham	L	2-4
24		Puppets	Jagendorf	A L C	3-5
49		Rhythms	Hughes	A sl L C CS	2-4
55		Roads	Bothwell	L	3-5
136		Sailing	M Lineaweaver	L C CS	8 up
31		Science Experiments	Wyler	A sl L C	4-6

No.	Title	Author	Key	Grade
57	Sea Shells	Cavanna	A L C	3-6
100	Ships	Bendick	A L C CS	3-6
23	Snakes	J Hoke	A sl L C CS H	3 up
124	Sound	Knight	A sl L	4 up
141	South America	Carter	A L	4 up
91	The Soviet Union	Snyder	A sl L C CS	5-8
34	Space Travel	Bendick	A sl L C CS	4-7
20	Stage Costume	Berk	A sl L C CS H	5 up
171	Stone Age Man	Dickinson	New Publication	
7	Stones	Cormack	A sl L C CS H	4 up
36	Submarines	Icenhower	A sl L C CS H	4 up
56	Supermarkets	Bendick	A sl L C CS	1-4
86	The Supreme Court	Coy	A sl L C	6 up
71	Surprising Facts	Chrystie	A sl L	2-5
127	Swimming	Schiffer	A sl L	2-5
120	Tales of Ancient Araby	Mozley	L	k-3
121	Tales of Ancient Egypt	Mozley	A L CS	k-3
144	Teaching Machines	Epstein	A sl L	7 up
59	Television	Stoddard	A sl L C	4-8
126	Tools	Liberty	A L	3-5
3	Trains	R Hamilton	A L C CS	3-6
17	Trees	Cormack	A sl L C CS H	3 up
78	Tropical Mammals	H Hoke	A L	4-7
106	The United Nations	E Epstein	A L C CS	4 up
147	Vikings	Rich	A sl L	4 up
145	War of 1812	Morris	A	5 up
138	Washington, D. C.	Epstein	L	5 up
117	Water	F C Smith	A L C	3-5
32	The Weather	Wyler	A L C CS	4-7
93	West Germany	Lobsenz	A sl L C	5-8
70	The West Indies	Hughes	A sl L C CS H	4 up
132	Wild Flowers	Cavanna	A sl L	4-6
52	Words	S & B Epstein	A sl L C CS	5-8
82	World War I	Snyder	A sl L C CS	6 up
80	World War II	Snyder	A sl L C CS	6 up

The FIRST BOOK Editions

No.	Title	Author	Key	Grade
E1	The Declaration of Independence		A L CS	All
E2	The Man Without a Country	Hale	A sl CS	All
E3	The Star Spangled Banner		A	All
E4	A Message to Garcia	Hubbard	New Publication	

ALL are supplied in the Watts Guaranteed Library Binding

ALL are in large, clear type

ALL are fully illustrated—many with over 100 pictures, and in color

ALL checked and double-checked for accuracy, authority, and clarity of text

ALL 7¼ x 8¾ size

ALL at one price

KEY TO LISTINGS:

- **A** American Library Association, Booklist
- **sl** Booklist, Small Library Listing
- **L** Library Journal
- **C** H. W. Wilson Company, Children's Catalog
- **CS** Child Study Association of America, Books of the Year for Children
- **H** H. W. Wilson Company, High School Catalog

Write for catalog. Address Dept. Sc

FRANKLIN WATTS, INC.
A Division of Grolier Incorporated
575 Lexington Avenue   New York 22, N. Y.

What they say about
FIRST BOOKS

"Their wide appeal, their broad coverage of varied subject areas, their wide range of significant and timely topics, and their attractive format and illustrations have made them valuable library materials."

MIRIAM PETERSON
Chicago Board of Education

"The format of each book has been superior and the books show that careful attention has been given to design, type, illustration, paper, and binding."

CAROLYN W. FIELD
Philadelphia Public Library

"I have long felt that the FIRST BOOKS developed (by Franklin Watts) were among the important creative contributions made by a publisher in recent decades."

PROF. HAROLD G. SHANE
Indiana University

"I really don't know how we ever ran our school libraries without the FIRST BOOKS!"

ELIZABETH HODGES
Baltimore Board of Education

"In covering a topic thoroughly, these books are like a junior encyclopedia, with an illustrated volume for each subject."

Christian Science Monitor

"Indeed an achievement! The high quality which has been maintained throughout the series is even more remarkable."

RUTH HILL VIGUERS
The Horn Book

"The FIRST BOOKS have made a real contribution in extending the horizons of their readers beyond the interests they knew they had."

JOSETTE FRANK
Child Study Association of America

28